Musings and all

Matutina

BookLeaf
Publishing

India | USA | UK

Presentation by *BookLeaf Publishing*

Web: www.bookleafpub.com

E-mail: info@bookleafpub.com

ISBN: 978-93-5761-171-8

First edition 2022

DEDICATION

To you. Thank you. For without you I would not be able to feel what I ought to feel. Thank you.

PREFACE

It's always been my dream to have a published book. What I have written here are collections of my past writings at the time when my heart was full of different kinds of emotions. It somehow helped me express myself and get to know myself better. This book is like looking into my soul at a time when I am at my lowest. A time when I was vulnerable. I hope i could tap you in one way or another as you read this book.
Thank you.

To Rhaine, my friend, thank you for hearing me out.

To all my friends whom I have bothered,thank you.

What is love?

When you love someone you have to give
everything that you can offer.

Give until you don't have anything to give.

Fight until the war is not yet over.

Love until love itself wears off.

Love until there is nothing left of you.

Because Loving yourself is also fighting for
what you feel and what makes you happy.

Pain

I am here once again pouring my heart out.

I am in pain.

I thought I was past that stage but I was wrong.

I can still feel it.

It still pierces my heart.

I can feel my heart squeeze.

My tears want to fall but i tried not to.

When will this stop?

I am tired.

Death

And I wonder how long will I live?

How long will I endure living?

A life without purpose.

A life with nothing but an empty heart and empty soul.

Walking without direction.

Running away from life.

Leaning towards something that isn't for me.

How long?Oh how long will it last?

Me

And everyday I think of you.

I wonder if you think of me too.

Do you still love me as a lover or only just as a friend?

You have your own life.

The ones we dreamed of before are now coming true.

Only, not with me.

I hope you are happy.

I pray you find yourself and your peace.

I love you. And I don't know if Ican still love another.

I will keep writing till I have nothing to write.

But now...

Just let me be..

You

My heart is tired. I am tired.
I am trying to pull myself together.
I feel so alone. I feel empty.

I pray. Day and night and in between.
God has been my companion. My constant. I
talk to Him.

I pray that He will help you be okay.

I want you to have the Peace that you need.

I want you to be happy. I really do.

Even if it means that I will no longer be by your
side.

I really want the best for you.

Please be okay.

At least one of us is okay. Is happy. Is at peace.

Pls let it be you.

Stuck

I love you.

I always say that to you.

But you don't love me anymore.

It hurts. It pains me.

But I can't do anything about it.

I want you to love me again.

I want to bring back the past.

But I can't do it alone.

I want you to feel my love.
My love overflows for you. That no matter what
you do. I will always love you.

This feeling that Ihave, I don't know if it will
ever fade.

I hope it does. But I guess it won't.

I'm afraid that I will be stuck in this emotion. I am afraid that I will never get over you.

I'm scared. That you have moved on and I still can't.

Thoughts of you

I am afraid when I am alone not because I am scared of ghosts but because I am afraid of my thoughts.

It redirects to you.

It is programmed to think of you.

It misses you.

And it is heartbreaking thinking of you.

Unlove or not?

How can i unlove you? How can I not miss you?
Maybe it's too early now. Maybe I won't be able
to get over you.

This love. The way I love, it's different. I love
like no other can. Can you not feel it?

Maybe there is a love that never dies. Maybe
this love dies together with me.

Over

And i asked how you feel?

You said that I should let you go.
To find myself. As I am not meant for you. And you are not meant for me.

And it felt real. It seems so honest. As for you to say that. To say that we are not meant to be.

That it is over.

Today I feel that it is over.

The now!

Living the now is just like me living in the past.

Was stagnant.

Was still.

Was nothing.

If one could enter my deep soul.

It would leave him chaos and uncertain.

There is no definite.

Always unsure.

Always second plans.

Wishing for something and hoping for another.

Days gone by and it is still the same.

Nothing changed.

Steadfast life.

Bleeding past.

Daunting future.

Why?

Why must someone get hurt?

Why must I be the only one hurting?

Why must I cry all the time?

All i did was to love someone.Is it a curse to love you?

Will all the people who love you get hurt?

Why must you punish me?

Enlightening

CONFUSION will heal you.

DOUBTS will mold you.

PAIN will mend you.

Bewildered

Let us go to a place where everything is uncertain.

 Coz that is what we are.

Confusing. Unreal. Vague. Indefinite. Unclear.

Broken lines.

We are running in circles where the other one is walking fast and the other is moving in slow pace.

Hearts that never met.

Minds that are disarrayed.

Emotions kept hidden.

Present inconsistent.

Future unsure

☐ Surviving
☐

So this is what it is.

The feeling of being stabbed straight into your heart.

There are no warnings.

And if even you saw it coming, you can't move yourself to avoid the knife.

You just stand there, anticipating and expecting that it won't hurt you.

But then it did.

And that's when you realized that you need some help.

You need to live and you need to survive.

Waiting..

And after everything.

When will You give me the one thing that I most desire?

Been waiting patiently.

How do I know if it will still come?

Should I give up already?

Should I just let it go?

Just accept that there are things that are really not meant for you to have.

Been so lonely.

Been tired.

Been so hopeless.

Been empty.

Been nothing.

Been free but not free.

Been and still waiting..

Timeline

Everybody has its own timeline.

Maybe now is my season to grieve and to be hurt.

But there will come a time that I will be in decades of love, peace and happiness.

Just wait.

Be patient.

It will come.

Just believe.

Trust.

New Chapter

And when a new Chapter of life begins.

Where does the old one lie?

Is there a time when the forgotten past is significant at the present?

When love fades, where did it drift?

Can it still be found?

Re emerging

Out of the blue you came.

Everything felt the same.

It was quiet.

No drama.

Feelings unchanged.

But within my core, it isn't the old me.

I have changed

Caged

My heart bleeds for you.

It aches knowing you are not free.

Why must you do this?

Why must you put yourself in a cage?

Why do you have to let things get worse?

Have you not learned anything?As much as I want to understand you. I just can't put any logic to it.

Why? Why must you put yourself into this kind of situation over and over again?

New kind of love

I'm gonna find love or love will find me.

And it's gonna be a happy one.

Drama free kind of relationship.

Smooth one.

Stress free partnership.

Mutual admiration and mutual respect.

That's my kind of love now.

The peaceful and quiet type.

No extraordinary fireworks.

But a boring, satisfied, cuddly and sweet one.

That would be the greatest love of all.

The dream

I want to live in a place where no one knows me.
To be able to express myself without inhibitions.
To do everything that I want to do.

To find myself in a crowd.

To know what I really desire without no one to
choose for me.

To live alone but still not feeling alone.

To laugh at my mistakes and not think about
what others would say.

To express my love to someone without thinking
who makes the first move.

To appreciate myself without anyone comparing
me to someone else.

To be able to do wild things and not regret what
will happen after.

To be someone who will not please someone to
accept me as a person.

And lastly, to be someone whom I will be happy
with because I am me.

www.ingramcontent.com/pod-product-compliance
Lightning Source LLC
La Vergne TN
LVHW021350200726
843509LV00014B/2779